Amazing Inventions

Inventing GPS

by Kristi Lew

21:46

0,3   Main street, 21

150

FOCUS
READERS.

BEACON

www.focusreaders.com

Focus Readers is distributed by North Star Editions:
sales@northstareditions.com | 888-417-0195

Produced for Focus Readers by Red Line Editorial.

Photographs ©: Shutterstock Images, cover, 1, 6, 8, 11, 13, 16, 19, 22, 25, 26, 29; iStockphoto, 4, 21; MSFC/NASA, 14–15

Library of Congress Cataloging-in-Publication Data
Library of Congress Cataloging-in-Publication Data is available on the Library of Congress website.

ISBN
978-1-63739-047-4 (hardcover)
978-1-63739-101-3 (paperback)
978-1-63739-206-5 (ebook pdf)
978-1-63739-155-6 (hosted ebook)

Printed in the United States of America
Mankato, MN
012022

About the Author

Kristi Lew is a science educator living in St. Petersburg, Florida. She has written more than 65 books for students and teachers. Before becoming an author, she taught high school science and worked in genetics laboratories. When she's not writing, she likes to travel. She uses GPS to find her way.

Table of Contents

Chapter 1

Finding the Way

A soccer team has a game in another town. The coach will drive the players there in a van. She has never been to the town before. But that is not a problem.

A map app uses a smartphone's location to give directions.

Driving South on Maplecrest Dr

434

0.5ⁿ

Speed
0.0 m h

Menu

Driving
S

People can buy GPS units to use in their cars.

The coach opens a map **app** on her smartphone. She types the address of the soccer field. Then she taps to get directions. A player holds the phone while the coach drives. The phone tells her where to turn. It even says what time they will arrive.

The coach's phone is using GPS. This system tracks where the phone is. It uses this location to tell the coach how to get to the game.

Did You Know?

GPS stands for Global Positioning System. A device can use GPS to find its position anywhere in the world.

Chapter 2

Creating GPS

GPS helps people find where they are. It can also show them which way to go. GPS uses signals from **satellites**. The satellites **orbit** Earth.

 GPS helps people find their way while hiking or traveling.

The first satellite was launched in 1957. It wasn't part of GPS. But it sent radio waves back to Earth. The **frequency** of these waves changed as the satellite moved toward or away from the ground. This gave scientists an idea. They could use radio waves to track satellites. They could also find and track objects on Earth.

People began using satellites for **navigation** in the 1960s. These satellites helped the US Navy track

Radar is another navigation tool. It uses sound waves to find the positions of objects.

submarines. Soon after, the US Air Force made a similar system.

In the 1970s, the US military began working on Navstar. This system would use many satellites.

The first satellite launched in 1978. The last launched in 1993. But the system worked before then. It became known as GPS.

At first, only the military could use GPS. Then in 1983, US airlines were allowed to use GPS. By 1989, **civilians** could buy small GPS units.

Did You Know?

GPS is still owned by the US government. But it works all over the world.

 Some countries have their own satellite-based navigation systems. Russia has GLONASS.

People continued improving GPS throughout the 2000s. It became more **accurate**. It became easier to use. GPS also became less expensive.

Launching a Satellite

Scientists use rockets to send GPS satellites to space. To reach space, a rocket must overcome Earth's **gravity**. To do this, the rocket goes very fast. It goes more than 25,000 miles per hour (40,000 km/h).

When the rocket is high enough, it lets go of the satellite. The satellite's speed makes it move forward. But gravity pulls it toward Earth. These two forces work against each other. They keep the satellite in orbit. The satellite moves in a curve around Earth.

The rockets that launch GPS satellites hold lots of fuel.

USAF
MDA
JCWS

DELTA

NAVSTAR

MCDONNELL DOUGLAS

GPS NAVSTAR

Rockwell International

U.S. AIR FORCE

15

Chapter 3

How GPS Works

GPS is made up of three parts. It uses satellites, ground stations, and receivers. There are 31 GPS satellites. Each satellite orbits Earth twice a day.

 GPS satellites send and receive signals as they orbit Earth.

The satellites work as a group. Their paths form a pattern. Scientists plan each satellite's path carefully. They make sure satellites don't crash into one another.

Ground stations track each satellite's location. They track how fast it's moving, too. The stations make sure each satellite is in the

Did You Know?

GPS satellites orbit nearly 12,550 miles (20,200 km) above Earth's surface.

Ground stations around the world pick up radio waves sent by satellites.

right place. If it's not, they alert the master control station.

Scientists at that station find what's causing the problem. They write instructions to fix it. Then they send these changes up to the satellite.

A GPS receiver picks up signals from at least four satellites. It uses the signals to find its own location. It measures the time each signal takes to reach it. It also finds how far it is from that satellite. The receiver combines these numbers to figure out where it is on Earth. The

Did You Know?

Some GPS receivers are sold on their own. Others are part of vehicles or other devices.

GPS Signals

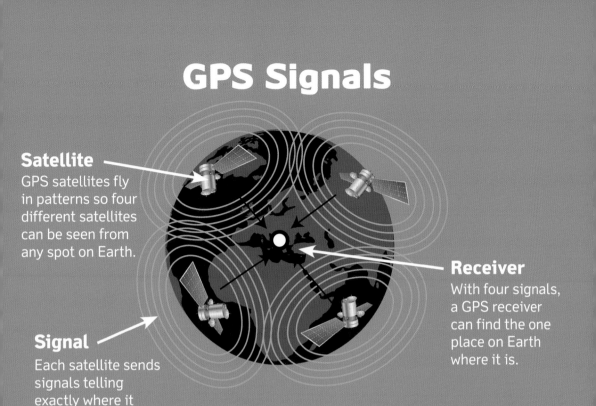

Satellite
GPS satellites fly in patterns so four different satellites can be seen from any spot on Earth.

Receiver
With four signals, a GPS receiver can find the one place on Earth where it is.

Signal
Each satellite sends signals telling exactly where it is and what time it's there.

more satellites it uses, the more accurate this location can be.

Many GPS receivers can also give directions. They can find a route from one place to another.

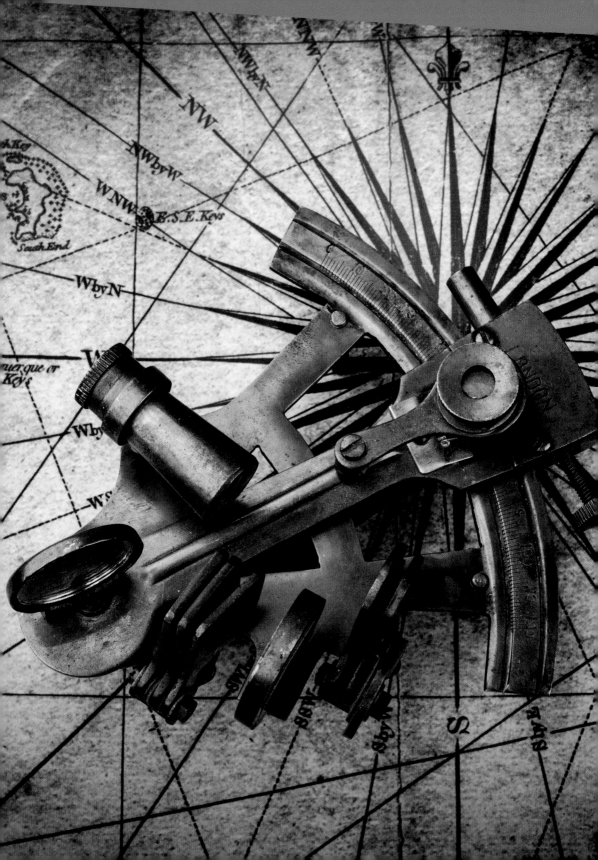

Chapter 4

What GPS Does

Before GPS, people often used maps and stars to navigate. Maps showed where stars were in the sky. People measured the angle between the stars and the **horizon**. They used it to find their location.

 A sextant was a tool that helped people calculate their location based on objects in the sky.

People also used **radar**. But these methods could be tricky to use.

Today, GPS helps people find their way quickly and easily. It's built into most computers, smartphones, and cars. People can get directions while hiking. Or they can search for the closest store. GPS also tracks ships and airplanes.

People even use GPS for fun. One example is geocaching. In this game, people hunt for treasure

 After finding a geocache box, a person signs the logbook. Its pages track who has found the box.

boxes. Websites list the boxes' locations. People use GPS to find them.

Scientists use GPS as well. They use it to study and track animals.

 Collars with GPS tags help scientists track the movements of wild animals.

GPS also helps people track storms. It can show where and how fast the storms are moving. Scientists can warn people to get to safety.

GPS helps provide error-free timing, too. All GPS satellites carry atomic clocks. These clocks measure time very exactly. They help do jobs where even small errors could cause huge problems. For example, they help people fly spacecraft. People all over the world rely on GPS.

Did You Know?

Banks use atomic clocks to track the exact times payments happen.

FOCUS ON
Inventing GPS

Write your answers on a separate piece of paper.

1. Write a letter to a friend that describes the main ideas from Chapter 3.

2. Would you want to try geocaching? Why or why not?

3. How many satellites does a GPS receiver use to find its location?
   - A. only one
   - B. at least four
   - C. two or three

4. What would happen if the GPS satellites stopped sending signals?
   - A. The satellites would stop orbiting Earth.
   - B. GPS receivers wouldn't be able to find their locations.
   - C. The master control station would have to move.

5. What does **route** mean in this book?

*Many GPS receivers can also give directions. They can find a **route** from one place to another.*

    A. a time in the morning

    B. a way to cook food

    C. a way to travel somewhere

6. What does **errors** mean in this book?

*These clocks measure time very exactly. They help do jobs where even small **errors** could cause huge problems.*

    A. places that don't exist

    B. measurements that are incorrect

    C. people who are in space

Answer key on page 32.

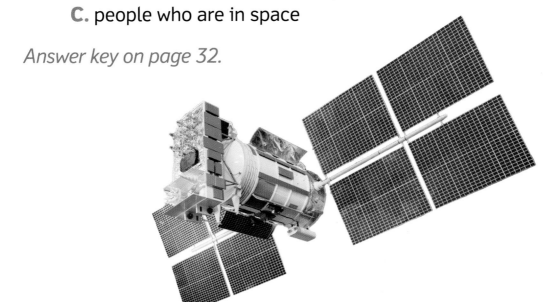

Glossary

accurate
True or correct.

app
A computer program that completes a task.

civilians
People who are not in the military.

frequency
The number of cycles per second that a radio wave has.

gravity
The natural force that pulls objects toward Earth.

horizon
The line where the sky and the ground seem to meet.

navigation
Skills or strategies used to find one's way while traveling.

orbit
To repeatedly follow a curved path around another object because of gravity.

radar
An instrument that locates things by bouncing radio waves off them.

satellites
Devices that orbit Earth.

To Learn More

BOOKS

Aschim, Hans. *How to Go Anywhere (and Not Get Lost): A Guide to Navigation for Young Adventurers.* New York: Workman Publishing, 2021.

Bell, Samantha S. *Road Maps and GPS.* Mankato, MN: The Child's World, 2019.

LaPierre, Yvette. *Inside GPS.* Minneapolis: Abdo Publishing, 2019.

NOTE TO EDUCATORS

Visit **www.focusreaders.com** to find lesson plans, activities, links, and other resources related to this title.

Index

A
atomic clocks, 27

D
directions, 6, 21, 24

G
geocaching, 24–25
ground stations, 17–19

M
map app, 6
master control station, 19
military, 10–12

N
navigation, 10, 23
Navstar, 11

R
radar, 24
radio waves, 10
receivers, 17, 20–21
rockets, 14

S
satellites, 9–12, 14,
   17–21, 27
smartphones, 6–7, 24

U
US Air Force, 11
US Navy, 10